WHALES
& DOLPHINS

WHALES
& DOLPHINS

TOM JACKSON

amber
BOOKS

Published by Amber Books Ltd
United House
North Road
London
N7 9DP
United Kingdom

www.amberbooks.co.uk
Instagram: amberbooksltd
Facebook: amberbooks
Twitter: @amberbooks
Pinterest: amberbooksltd

ISBN: 978-1-83886-424-8

Project Editor: Anna Brownbridge
Designer: Keren Harragan
Picture Research: Terry Forshaw

Printed in China

Contents

Introduction

The story of the whales and dolphins almost defies belief. Their closest living relatives are the hippos, and they form a group of mammals called Cetacea that have left the land and returned to a life in the sea. They never come on dry land purposefully, and all 94 species have completely lost their hind limbs. Only the tell-tale hip bones remain in the sleek abdomen, which instead terminates with a wide and flattened tail made from two fleshy flukes. The

forelegs are now paddle-shaped pectoral fins. While the tail provides propulsion, these side fins are used for steering. In an incredible example of convergent evolution, whales and dolphins mostly have a third, dorsal fin on the back, something much more fish than furry beast. The dorsal fin is there to stop the creature from rolling as it moves forward. Despite a certain fishiness, cetaceans dominate in one area like no other marine creature: sound. The smaller species are experts at echolocation. The larger ones sing to each other, sending hypnotic, lilting calls that travel hundreds of kilometres through the water.

ABOVE:
An orca, or killer whale, is a perfect mix of strength and agility.

OPPOSITE:
A mother Bryde's whale and her little calf feast together on a school of anchovies in the Gulf of Thailand. Increasingly, giant whales in this region struggle to find enough fish to eat.

Whales

Everyone knows what a whale is, don't they? These mighty marine mammals are certainly among the most familiar of all animals, but the term whale can still confuse. The word in English is derived from a most ancient term that refers to a "large sea creature". So, no confusion there. However, the term can be muddled across the cetaceans as a whole, with larger relatives of the dolphins attracting the term "whale". However, these creatures are dwarfed by the true owners of the name "whale", which make up the biggest animals around and include the largest and heaviest species of all time: the blue whale.

The size of a blue whale is hard to imagine. A human could swim through its major blood vessels. Its heart is the size of a three-door hatchback, and its tongue alone weighs 2.5 tonnes (2500kg). The blue whale is the head of the Balaenopteridae family, better known as the rorquals. The rorquals also include the humpback, grey, fin and sei whales. They are joined by relatives from a side family, the Balaenidae, which include the right whales and bowhead. Together, these two groups form the baleen whales. The baleen whales are toothless, gentle giants of the ocean that sieve out their fish and plankton food from gargantuan mouthfuls of water. They do so using a curtain of feathery baleen plates that hang from the gums. Plankton offers a meagre meal, and this life requires economies of scale. Only a vast animal like a whale can be sustained this way.

OPPOSITE:
Into the blue
An immense blue whale turns its 25m (82ft) body to the deep and swims down into the dark.

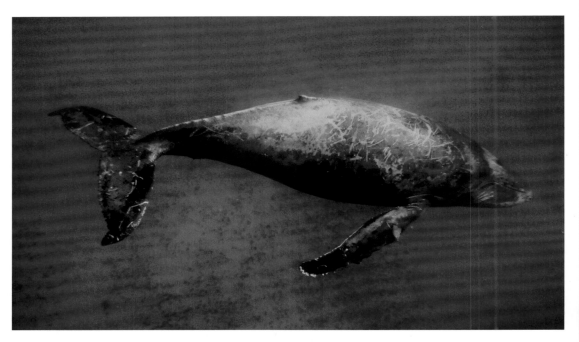

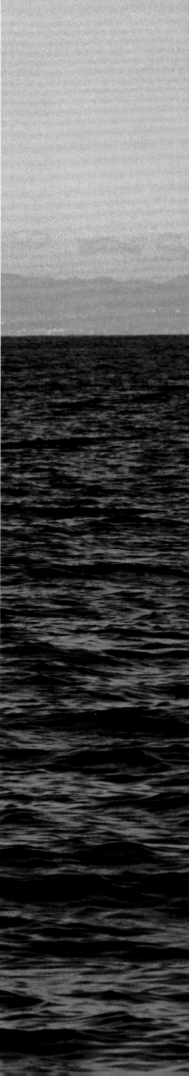

ABOVE TOP:
Battle scars
This adult blue whale is covered with pale scars. This suggests that the animal is older and has seen many a fight with orcas and sharks. Those predators could not take down an adult blue whale but may have been after its calves.

ABOVE BOTTOM:
On the move
Most populations of blue whales migrate and are constantly on the move. The whale's steady swimming speed is around 22km/h (13.7mph), but when alarmed a blue whale can hit 48 km/h (29.8mph).

RIGHT:
Lunge
A blue whale breaks the surface with a lunge. Unlike in a breach, the whole whale does not clear (or mostly clear) the water in a lunge. It looks like this whale is taking a mouthful of krill shoaling at the surface.

Fluking
A blue whale raises its tail flukes out of the water as it begins a steep dive. The tail is made from fleshy flukes which combine to a width of 7.5m (24.6ft) – the size of a minibus!

Spout
The water spout puffed from the blue whale's nostril-like blowholes rises 10m (32.8ft) above the surface. The whale's spout typically has a teardrop shape. Also visible is this giant species' small dorsal fin, which is a meagre 35cm (13.8in) tall.

Antarctic minke whale
At around 9m (29.5ft) long, this is
one of the smaller rorquals. The
upright dorsal fin is about two-
thirds of the way down the back.
It is more curved than those of
larger whales and resembles that
of a dolphin.

Antarctic minke whale
This krill-scooping species feeds mostly along the edge of the ice sheet in the Southern Ocean. It is a distinct species that is completely isolated from its Arctic cousin.

ABOVE AND OPPOSITE:
Bowhead whale
Although not the longest species, this Arctic species is one of the heaviest at 100 tonnes (100000kg). It feeds close to or under ice using its huge mouth (about a third of the length of the body as a whole) to filter out zooplankton. Its blubbery body keeps out the cold and can smash through 1m (3.3ft) of ice to make breathing holes.

Bryde's whale
For many years, this species was seen as a type of sei whale that lived in tropical waters. Migrating less than other whales to follow foods, this species targets a wide range of fish. It blows a spiral of "bubble nets" around a shoal so they bunch up into mouth-sized balls near the surface. Although no one has figured out if or how they cooperate, Bryde's whales often feed in groups.

Baleen

The largest cetaceans, around 15 species, are known as baleen whales. This term refers to the sieve-like filters they use to strain foods – everything from fish to microplankton – from mouthfuls of water. The filters are made from feathery keratin called baleen plates. Keratin – a tough but flexible material also found in fingernails and hair – was once better known as "whalebone".

Common minke whale

The smallest of all rorquals, this Arctic whale is breaching clear of the water. The origin of the name is not clear. It is perhaps named after a mythical Norwegian sailor who was forever misidentifying these small whales for more lucrative giants. This "small" 9m (29.5ft) species is more commonly seen near the Arctic coasts.

Fin whale

Earth's second-largest animal species, the fin whale, reaches around 20m (65.6ft) in length – a few metres short of the blue whale. However, it is perhaps half the weight or less of its superlative cousin. Its long and slender body has been likened to a racing yacht, and this fin whale is one of the most widespread whales, found sailing through all oceans.

Visible fin

Although the fin whale's dorsal fin is small in proportion to the bulk of its body, it is a tall feature for a whale of this size. Reaching just 70cm (27.6in) in height, this is nevertheless the biggest fin in the animal kingdom. The species name alludes to the way that the fin is seen soon after the animal surfaces to breathe out and is used as an identifying feature.

LEFT:
Meal time
The fin whale's underside, from the chin to the navel, has up to 100 pleats that allow the skin to expand enormously when gulping in a mouthful of water. Everything about giant whales is based on an economy of scale, and this lunge will bag the whale a mouthful holding 70m^3 (2472ft^3) of water.

ABOVE:
Krill
Shrimp-like crustaceans called krill are among the most common animals in the oceans. They are a mainstay of the diets of the largest whales. A fin whale will consume 2 tonnes (2000kg) of krill and other plankton every day.

ABOVE AND RIGHT:
Grey whale
Named for their grey skin, which is mottled further by pale scars left by parasites, this species of whale spends the year migrating up and down the Pacific coastlines. It is a favourite of whale spotters and gives a distinctive heart-shaped spout from its blowholes.

ALL PHOTOGRAPHS:
Fellow travellers
The grey whale appears especially prone to barnacles and other parasites that set up home on its skin. These grow in number when the whales are feeding in warm waters and then drop off as their hosts head into cold polar areas. The whales will breach the surface in an attempt to dislodge the more irritating stowaways.

OVERLEAF:
Bottom feeder
Grey whales feed at the seabed and are thus restricted to shallower coastal waters. The whale twists onto its side and scoops up the mud using its downturned mouth. It then filters out the silty water to get at the crustaceans and shellfish.

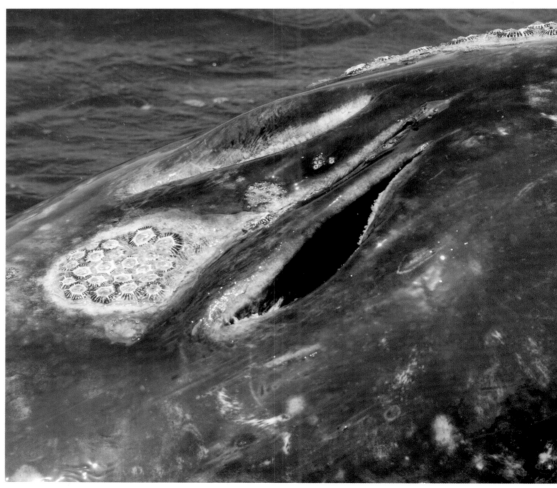

OPPOSITE:

Humpback

So named after the distinctive
double hump of its stumpy dorsal
fin, the humpback whale is also
distinctive for the bumpy tubercles
on its snout. These each surround
bristled hair and probably have
a sensory function, which is as
yet undefined.

ABOVE:

Flip over

In a move called a pec slap, this
humpback is rolling over to crash
its long pectoral fin on the surface.
This creates a distinctive sound
that communicates with other
whales nearby.

On show
Thanks to their frequent surfacing
behaviours, humpbacks are one of
the best species to observe in the
wild. They produce a short but
distinctively rounded spout.

Making a splash
The most exciting display from a humpback is the breach. Here, the whale surges vertically out of the water and rises into the air so that more than two-thirds of its immense body is above the surface. Next, the whale will actively twist and turn as it falls to maximize the crash and splash when it hits the water on its side. Stay back!

ABOVE:

Shallow dive

Humpbacks have distinctively serrated (almost tattered) trailing edges to their tail flukes. The tail is typically held above the water as the animal begins to dive. This high angle suggests the dive is on a shallow trajectory. The received wisdom is that the tail is held flatter to the surface before a deeper dive gets underway.

RIGHT:

Searching for scraps

Humpbacks cannot help but be messy eaters, and they mostly feed near to the surface. Here, some gulls have spotted the opportunity to snatch up some rather startled fish that have fallen out of the whale's mouth.

ALL PHOTOGRAPHS:

A calf

All whales give birth underwater, and the mother pushes the newborn up to the surface to take its first breath. The calf is fed a rich milk, all while underwater, and weaned after five months. The humpback whales live in families, so offspring and parents are always close by.

OPPOSITE AND LEFT:
Barnacles
Humpbacks are prone to infestations of barnacles – mostly acorn and gooseneck barnacles. They are more likely to collect these parasites, which are largely harmless, because they swim more slowly than other whales.

BELOW:
Breach baby
A young humpback with short stubby fins – unlike the wing-shaped flippers of the adults – tries out some breaching behaviour.

ALL PHOTOGRAPHS:
Feeding time
Humpback whales are mostly surface feeders using lunge attacks. They target shoals of krill (seen above pouring from the mouth) but also work as a team to corral schooling fish with bubble nets.

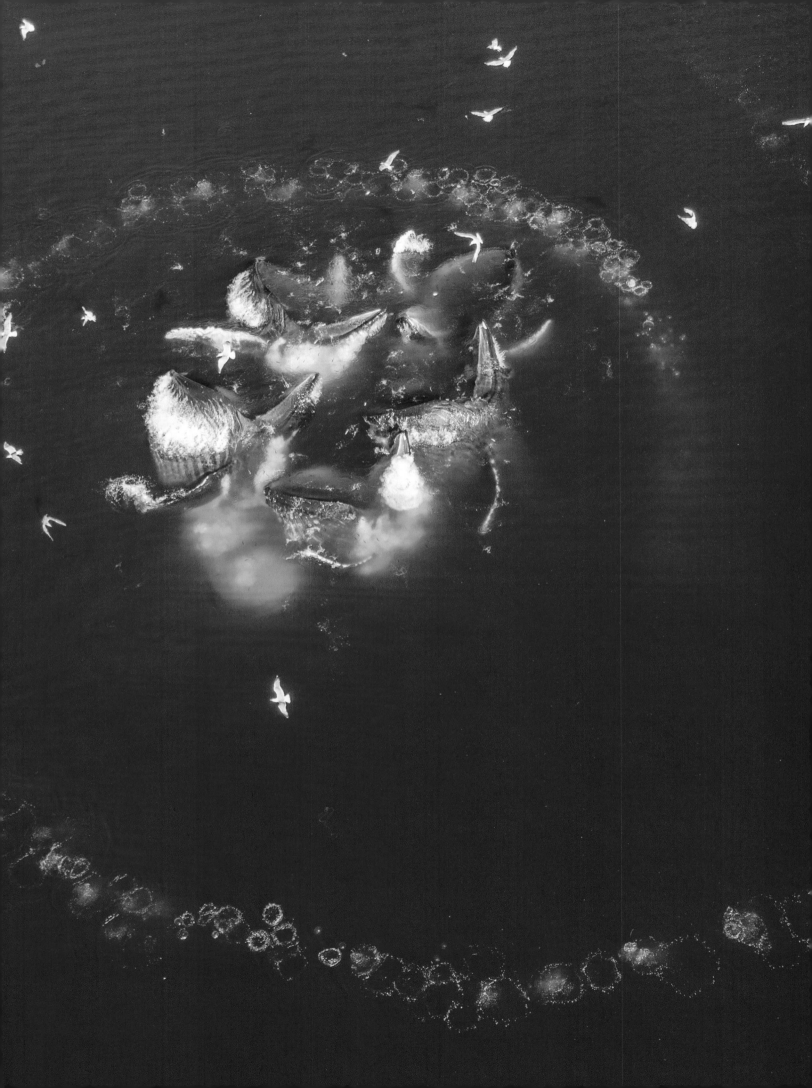

North Atlantic right whale
With just 350 individuals left, this species is the most endangered of the giant whales. The whales were named "right" because they were ideal for exploitation by whalers. Around 40 per cent of the body is oil-rich blubber, and once killed, the whale's carcass floats at the surface for easy salvage.

ABOVE:
Spyhop
A right whale pokes its head above the water just enough for its eye to clear the surface. It is taking a look around, scanning the horizon for landmarks (literally) and other whales in a common whale behaviour called spyhopping.

OPPOSITE:
Showing off
Right whales are a quiet and solitary bunch. They are seldom seen breaching or performing other surface behaviours other than to attract mates. This whale is breaching as part of a SAG, or surface active group, that has formed for breeding purposes.

Omura's whale

Also called the dwarf fin whale, this species is seldom seen outside of the Indo-Pacific region and was only described in 2003. It was the first of what is now called the Bryde's whale complex. In a species complex, the line between subspecies and species is very faint. Two newer members for the complex – Eden's whale and Rice's whale – have been proposed very recently.

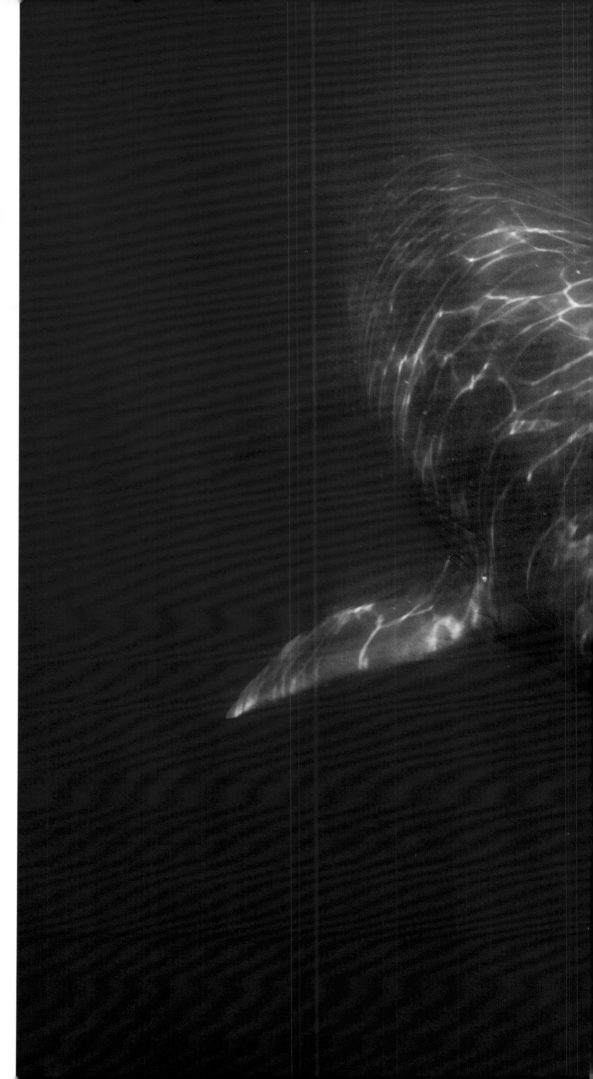

OPPOSITE:
Omura's whale
This species patrols the South
Seas and can sometimes be seen
migrating past Polynesian islands.
However, Omura's whales are
elusive creatures that seldom show
off at the surface.

ABOVE TOP AND BOTTOM:
Pygmy blue whale
The waters where the Indian and
Pacific Oceans meet the Southern
Ocean of Antarctica are home to
this subspecies of blue whale. The
maximum length of these whales
is 24m (78.7ft). The average length
of the blue whale subspecies is
around 20m (65.6ft), which still
makes these pygmies some of the
largest creatures on Earth.

Sei whale
This endangered species is the third largest whale in the world, being on average just a few centimetres shorter than the fin whales. The sei whale lives worldwide but avoids the warmer waters of the Indian Ocean and the cold polar seas.

ALL PHOTOGRAPHS:
Elusive character
The sei whale gets its name from the Norwegian word for pollock, a white fish of colder waters. In antiquity, fishermen noticed that these whales appeared along the Scandinavian coast at the same time as the pollock shoals. Otherwise, the often solitary whale is seldom seen. It is the fastest of the rorquals, with a top speed of 50km/h (31.1mph), and it rarely breaches or flukes. Often, the only available views of the sei whale are its arching back and fin sliding through the water.

ALL PHOTOGRAPHS:
Southern right whale
This Antarctic cousin of the two northern right whales – one in the Pacific, one in the Atlantic – is much more widespread and abundant. Genetic evidence suggests that Arctic and Antarctic right whales have not interbred for several million years.

LEFT AND ABOVE TOP:

Gnarly dude

Right whales have pale areas of rough skin on the head. These callosities are occupied by colonies of whale lice – a kind of crustacean not too distantly related to woodlice that grows to about 5mm (0.2in) in length. The whale and lice – several thousand per host – are in symbiosis. The lice do no harm to the whale but as far as we know offer no advantage either.

ABOVE BOTTOM:

A trip north

A southern right whale is visiting the coast of South Africa. This region of converging ocean currents is teeming with food. The southern right whale also ventures up to the coast of Australia and has been seen as far north as Tanzania and Brazil.

Dolphins

Everyone loves a dolphin. With their knowing glance and perpetually smiling faces, we cannot help but feel they are kindred spirits. Dolphins are indeed clever creatures. They have a huge brain, rivalling ours for size as a proportion of the body. The dolphins need a big brain to process all the sound information they rely on in the water. With no nose (despite their beaky looks), dolphins use their tongue to pick up scant chemical scents in the water. The eyes work above and below water but vision while submerged is a limited sense. Instead, dolphins rely on echolocation – a natural form of sonar – to detect distant objects and target prey. The initial high-pitched call is focused through a fatty "melon" bulging at the front of the head. This creates precisely calibrated beams of sound that are set up to probe into the distance, survey a school of fish and even stun a victim before attack. It is thought that dolphins can use their ultrasonic calls to scan the internal organs of sea animals. For example, they can detect the internal swim bladders of fish to discern particular types, and may also be able to pick up physiological information about other dolphins, thus gauging their moods and motivations. Perhaps they can read our emotions with their high-pitched squeaks, too.

Whatever they are doing, it works well. There are 44 species in four families that are found in all oceans and many of the world's greatest river systems. Nevertheless, many dolphins are in grave danger of extinction as humans continue to disturb the ocean's natural balance with fishing nets, engine noise and plastic pollution.

OPPOSITE:
Amazon river dolphin
The famed pink dolphins of the Amazon basin are found living in the foothills of the Andes, far from the nearest ocean.

LEFT:

Serene swimmers
Also known as botos, the Amazon river dolphins are slow swimmers, with a casual speed of 3km/h (1.9mph) and an escape velocity of just 20km/h (12.4mph). Nevertheless, they are often found in the deep pools above river rapids, which suggests they have the stamina to surge upstream against the intense currents.

OVERLEAF:

Water, water everywhere
The boto is the largest and most widespread of four river dolphins in the Amazon system. Together, these species – demoted to sub-species by some authorities – form the Iniidae family of dolphins. This part of the world is riddled with wide, river channels but also has vast areas of flood forests. There are plenty of places for the dolphins to live.

Changing colour

The Amazon river dolphins are born grey and steadily acquire their pink colouring as they age. The males are pinker than the females. This colour might help in "blackwater" systems where the water is clear but dark red-brown due to the chemicals leaching from the wood all around. Nevertheless, botos are also seen in whitewater habitats, where the water is murky with clays and mud.

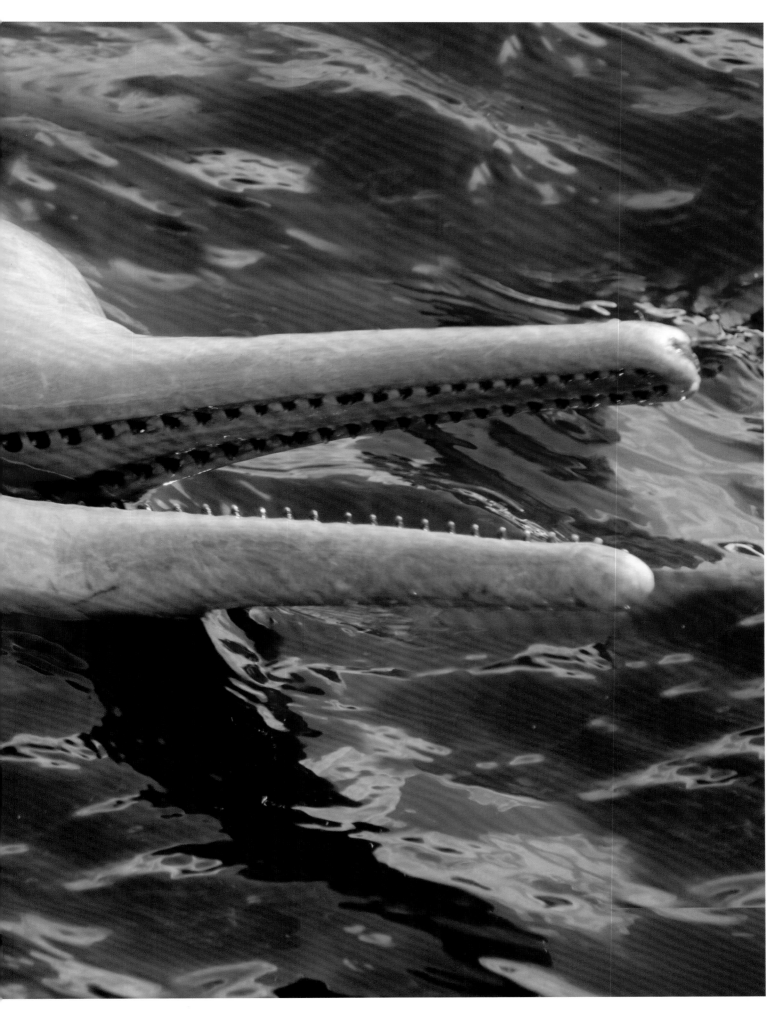

Atlantic spotted dolphin
This species is a common resident of the warmer seas in the Atlantic Ocean. It has a northern limit around the Grand Banks (a great place to find food) and a southernmost one near the River Plate.

LEFT:

Spot to adult
The Atlantic spotted dolphin only really develops its spots in adulthood. This is a younger dolphin with spots limited to the belly. The older adults are spotted all over.

ABOVE:

Atlantic white-sided dolphin
This dolphin species – at about 2.8m (9.2ft) long, it is an average-sized one – lives to the north of the spotted dolphin, heading into the fringes of the Arctic Ocean in summer.

Rear stripe
Despite the name, Atlantic white-sided dolphins have a distinctive pale brown or yellow stripe running on their flanks behind the dorsal fin. This coloured feature is not seen in other species. The belly is also mostly white or cream.

Australian humpback dolphin
This species is named after the double hump of its dorsal fin. Until recently, it was thought that there were just two species of humpback dolphins; one each for the Atlantic and Indian Oceans. However, over the last decade, the Indian Ocean species has been split in three: Australian, Indian Ocean and Indo-Pacific.

Australian snubfin dolphin
Another species named for its
distinctive dorsal fin anatomy,
this Australian dolphin hugs the
warm coastal waters of northern
Australia and New Guinea.
It is a recent offshoot of the
Irrawaddy dolphin, which has
a similar presence in and around
the peninsulas and islands of the
Indo-Malay region.

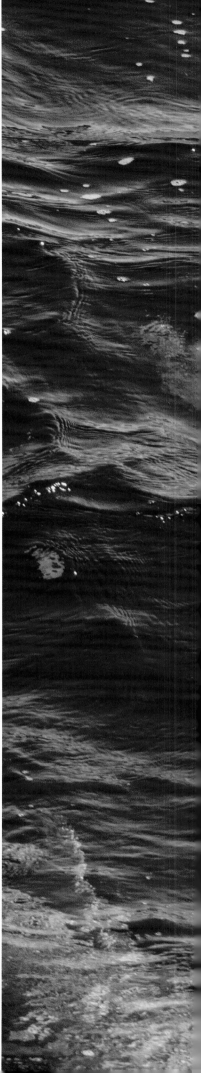

ALL PHOTOGRAPHS:
Clymene dolphin
Once known as the short-snouted spinner dolphin due to its habit of performing rolls in the air, this species lives in the equatorial Atlantic and the Caribbean Sea. They are found mostly in deep waters far from the coast.

OVERLEAF:
Subtle features
With its three-tone markings, from dark grey on the back to a paler pink-white on the belly, this species closely resembles the spinner dolphin. The defining difference is a shorter beak. As both species share the same region and hunt in the same places, the beak sizes probably reflect how each dolphin targets different types of fish.

BOTH PHOTOGRAPHS:
Commerson's dolphin
A resident of the water around Cape Horn and Tierra del Fuego, this sticky little species has a highly distinctive colouring, with a thick band of white between the black head and tail.

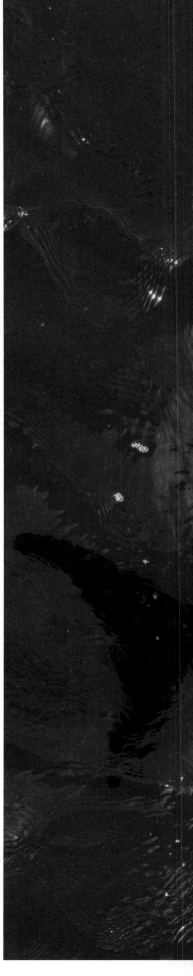

Keeping busy
Commerson's dolphin is a very
active species, moving between
shallow coasts and deeper water as
it follows shoals of fish and squid.
Many groups also snaffle shellfish
living on shallow sandy seabeds.

Common bottlenose dolphin
The world ambassador of dolphinkind, this species lives worldwide, avoiding only the coldest polar waters. It is big compared to most dolphins, with some males reaching 4m (13.1ft) long. Typically of dolphins, it has short, blunt, peg-like teeth, which are used to grip and hold slippery prey rather than stab and slice them.

ALL PHOTOGRAPHS:

Common bottlenose dolphin

Despite being the poster child for dolphins, the bottlenose species is quite unusual. It has a larger brain and has been shown to be more intelligent. It is able to learn simple languages, solve puzzles and have complex social interactions. These dolphins sometimes team up with fishing boats to find and capture shoals of fish.

OVERLEAF:

Common dolphin

Despite the name, this species is less widespread than other members of the oceanic dolphin family Delphinidae (numbering 37 species). Nevertheless, it is the most abundant of any dolphin species, with an estimated world population of six million.

ABOVE TOP:
Common dolphin
The common dolphin is represented in all non-polar oceans but is a rare sight in the Indian Ocean. Its main distributions are the North Pacific, North Atlantic (including the Mediterranean) and the Tasman Sea between Australia and New Zealand.

ABOVE BOTTOM:
Short-beaked
Most of the common dolphins are described as being short-beaked. They tend to dominate the deeper areas of the species's range, where they congregate around seamounts and other large-scale seafloor features.

RIGHT:
Long-beaked
The long-beaked common dolphins are mostly found in shallow and warmer coastal waters. Analysis shows that the long-beaked population is not genetically distinct from the short beaked, so although there is a measurable difference, they are both the same species.

False killer whale
Originally grouped with the orca, or killer whale, due to apparent similarities in skull anatomy, this was soon found to be a false relationship, hence the common name.

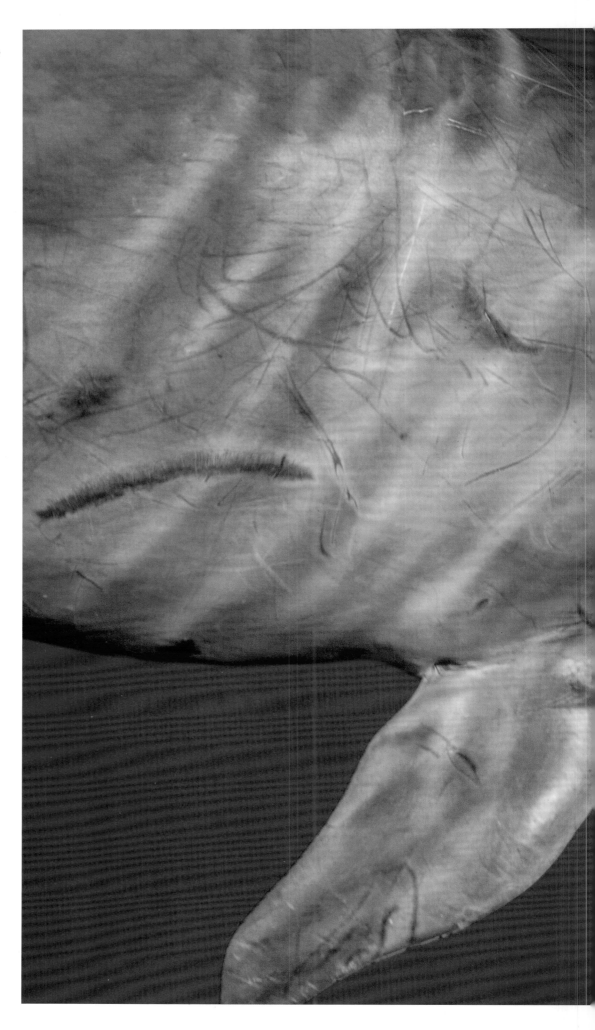

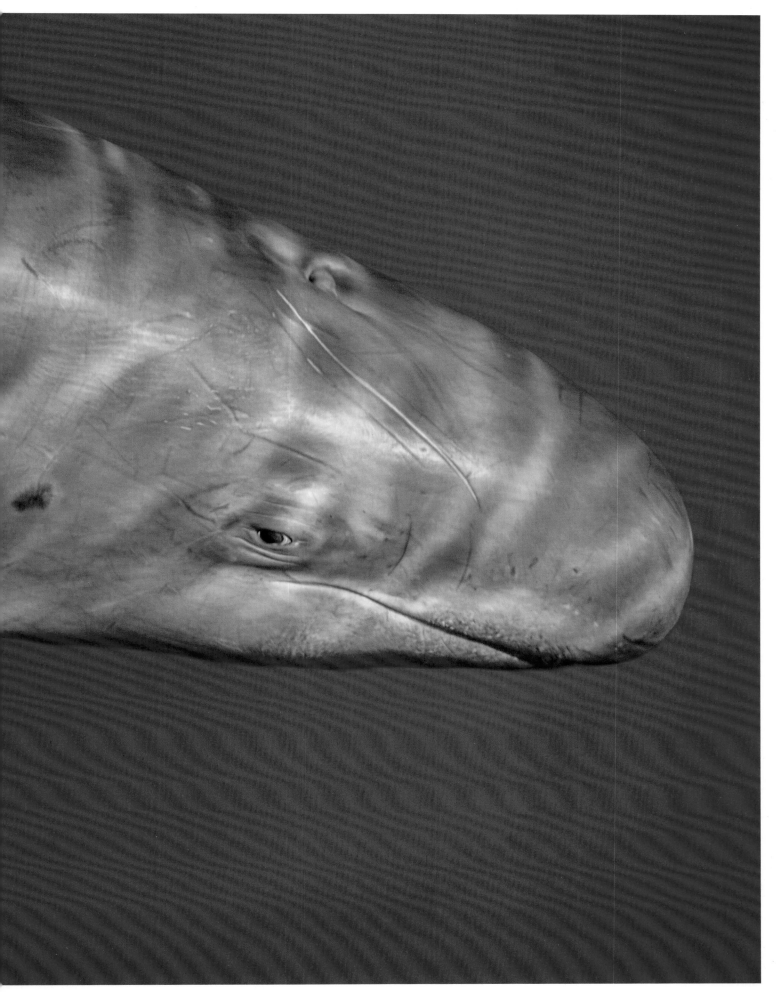

False killer whale

The false killer whale grows up to 6m (19.7ft) long. It lives along the continental shelves, where the waters are shallow and filled with life. The species is most common in warmer tropical waters, where it preys on large fish and also attacks other dolphins. Pods of false killer whales attack the calves of baleen whales.

Dusky dolphin
This small species from the coasts of South America and the waters around New Zealand is seen as a close relative of the more widespread Pacific white-sided dolphin. The dusky term refers to the darker markings found on this species.

ALL PICTURES:
Dusky dolphin
This species prefers coastal waters where cold currents are creating upwellings. These flows of deep water rising to the surface mix in nutrients and create the conditions for marine life to thrive.

OVERLEAF:
Fraser's dolphin
This large tropical dolphin feeds on the surface of deep waters. It can gather in huge superpods with many thousands of members.

Hector's dolphin

As its colouring shows, this dolphin is a relative of the Commerson's dolphin from South America. This rare species is restricted to the inland waters of New Zealand.

OPPOSITE BOTTOM:

Indian Ocean humpback dolphin

Located in the western coasts of the Indian Ocean, this species was only identified in 2014. Before that, it was thought to be a subspecies of the Indo-Pacific humpback dolphin.

ABOVE:

Ganges River dolphin

This is one of two species of freshwater dolphin in South Asia that form the Platanistidae family along with the Indus River dolphin. Both are endangered due to pollution and fishing nets. River habitats are also dramatically altered by dams and barrages built to control floods and make power.

Hourglass dolphin
This small species lives along the coasts of the Antarctic in the Southern Ocean. It strays north to the tip of South America. It feeds near the seabed and preys on squid, crustaceans and fish.

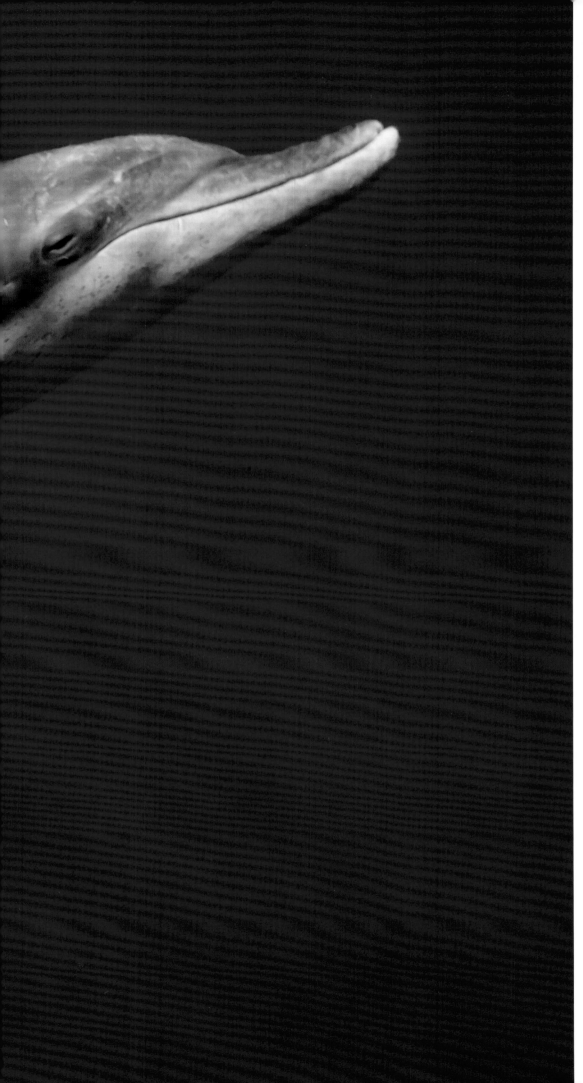

Indo-Pacific bottlenose dolphin
A close relative of the common bottlenose dolphin, this dolphin is found only in the coastal waters from Mozambique to Polynesia. The species is a little smaller than the common species, and it has a longer beak.

ALL PHOTOGRAPHS:
Indo-Pacific bottlenose dolphin
These smart, playful and gregarious dolphins rub themselves against corals and sponges. It is suggested that this behaviour might help them tackle irritated skin problems.

OVERLEAF:
Indo-Pacific humpback dolphin
The pink colouring of this dolphin indicates that this is an older individual. The grey skin becomes paler with age.

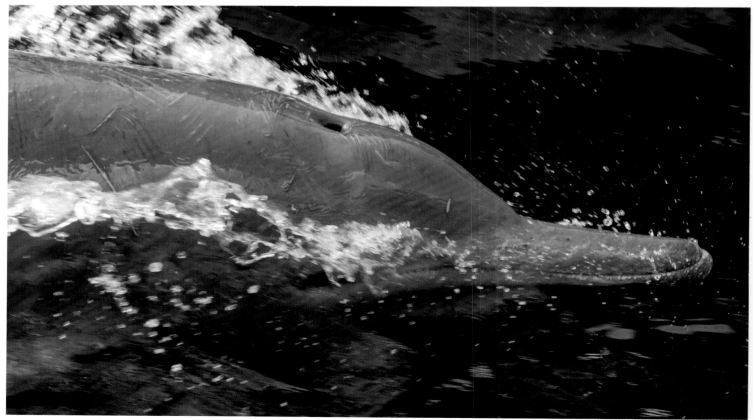

LEFT:

Indo-Pacific humpback dolphin
Targeting a wide range of prey in the South China Sea and Indo-Malay region, this species hunts in groups of around 10.

OPPOSITE BOTTOM:

Plastic risk
As a coastal species, the Indo-Pacific humpback dolphin is at risk from plastic pollution. The floating waste interferes with the dolphin's echolocation.

BELOW:

Irrawaddy dolphin
This endangered snubfin dolphin live along the coasts of Southeast Asia, where it ventures far up estuaries and coastal lagoons. Additionally, the dolphin is endemic in the Irrawaddy River.

RIGHT:
Long-finned pilot whale
Despite the name, this is a species of oceanic dolphin. It lives in the sub-Arctic waters and Southern Ocean. Its close relative, the short-finned pilot whale, lives in the waters in between. Both are highly social and prey on a wide range of fish, squids and crustaceans.

OVERLEAF:
Melon-headed whale
Also called the electra dolphin, or little killer whale, this oceanic dolphin lives in the deep areas of tropical and subtropical oceans. It is a rare sight and is most likely spotted around Pacific islands.

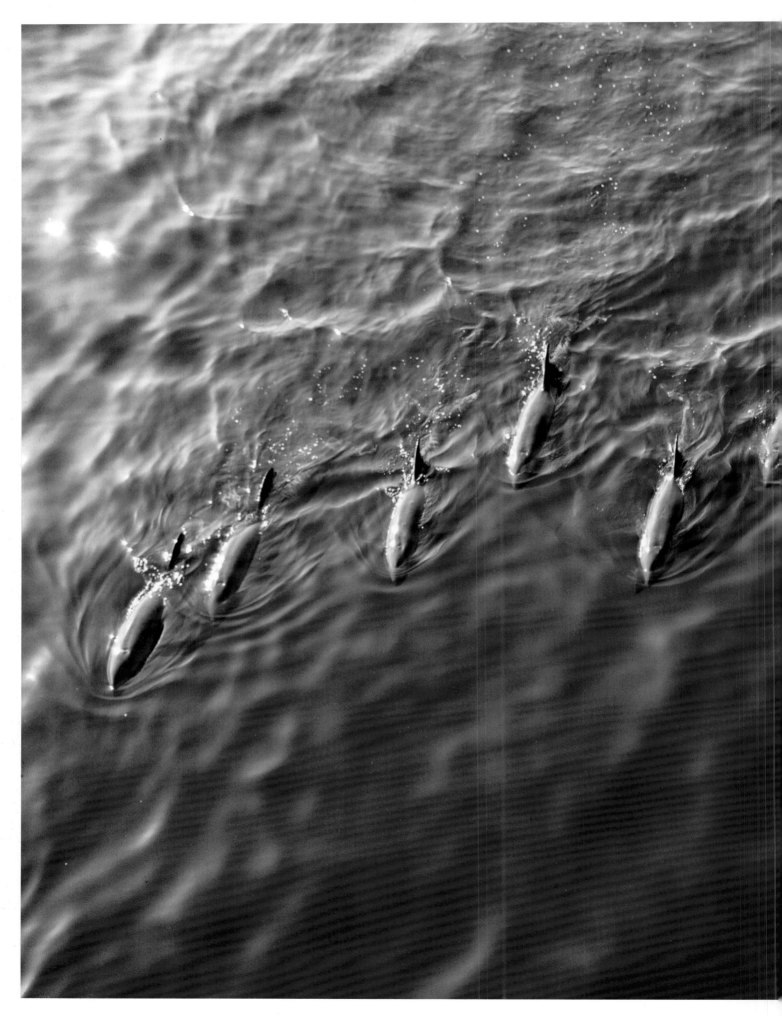

Melon-headed whale
This big dolphin generally travels in large groups of around 100, sometimes swelling into the thousands. They hunt in deep waters during the day to attack nocturnal predators. At night, these predatory fish and squid swim up to the surface and the melon-headed whales follow.

OPPOSITE TOP:

Northern right whale dolphin

This cetacean shares its Arctic range with the northern right whales, two of the largest baleen species. The dolphin's most obvious feature is a lack of dorsal fin.

OPPOSITE BOTTOM:

Fast mover

Despite being considerably smaller than its whale namesake, the northern right whale dolphin is one of the fastest dolphins, with a top speed of 40km/h (24.9mph). Pods porpoise or leap in and out of the water as they swim so they can breathe as they speed along.

LEFT:

Guiana dolphins

Also called the costero, this oceanic dolphin lives along the eastern coast of South America. It is one of the few that is able to swim habitually in and out of freshwater, and often probes up rivers. However, it does not go as far inland as its close relative and neighbour, the tucuxi.

Orca

Better known by its more lurid name of killer whale, this is the largest dolphin species. It reaches 9m (29.5ft) in length and has a top weight of 6 tonnes (6000kg), which is the same as an Africa bull elephant. The orca is not just an apex predator but perhaps the pre-eminent one. It eats the calves of all whale species and even kills great white sharks.

135

ABOVE TOP:
Unmistakable
The black and white body of the orca is hard to confuse with another species, and the great size is a sure confirmation. The back is mostly black and the underside is a contrasting white (including under the tail). There is a tell-tale saddle of white behind the dorsal fin.

ABOVE BOTTOM:
Follow mother
Orcas live in pods of about a dozen. The group is ruled by an older female, who is mother to many of the pod members. She remembers the best feeding grounds as conditions fluctuate year on year, and passes this knowledge on to her successor.

RIGHT:
Big mouth
Killer whales kill with an immense crushing bite rather than a bloody slice and slash of teeth. Pods appear to be specialized at exploiting different foods. Some target seals, other fish or cephalopods, and some target the calves of giant whales.

Wolves of the sea
A pack of orcas is the ultimate
marine force. The large dorsal fins,
considerably taller in the males,
are the only warning their prey
may get, and it is often too late.
On average, each orca eats 1 tonne
(1000kg) of food every week.

Pacific white-sided dolphin
Also known as the hookfin dolphin due to its curved dorsal fine, this cute species lives in the colder waters of the North Pacific Ocean. It is very active during the day and sleeps around seven hours at night, swimming slowly at the surface with an alternating half of the brain staying awake to stop the animal from drowning.

ABOVE:
Pantropical spotted dolphin
This medium-sized species is found in all the warm ocean waters of the world, as its name suggests. It is one of the most abundant species, thanks in part to the move to make tuna fishing "dolphin friendly". Many of these tropical dolphins were getting caught in the huge nets used to trap tuna but are spared by current methods.

RIGHT:
Round wounds
This pantropical spotted dolphin has a couple of round wounds inflicted by a cookie-cutter shark. This small, deep-sea shark swims nearer to the surface at night and chomps out discs of flesh from larger sea creatures using a twisting bite.

Peale's dolphin
A pod of these small dolphins from the waters around Cape Horn at the southern tip of South America takes turns riding a bow wave as it pays a visit to some human seafarers passing through its habitat.

Pygmy killer whale
This species is also known as the slender blackfish or the slender pilot whale. The rare and seldom-seen species shares some superficial similarities with orcas. At only 2m (6.6ft) long, this is the smallest animal to be habitually referred to as a whale.

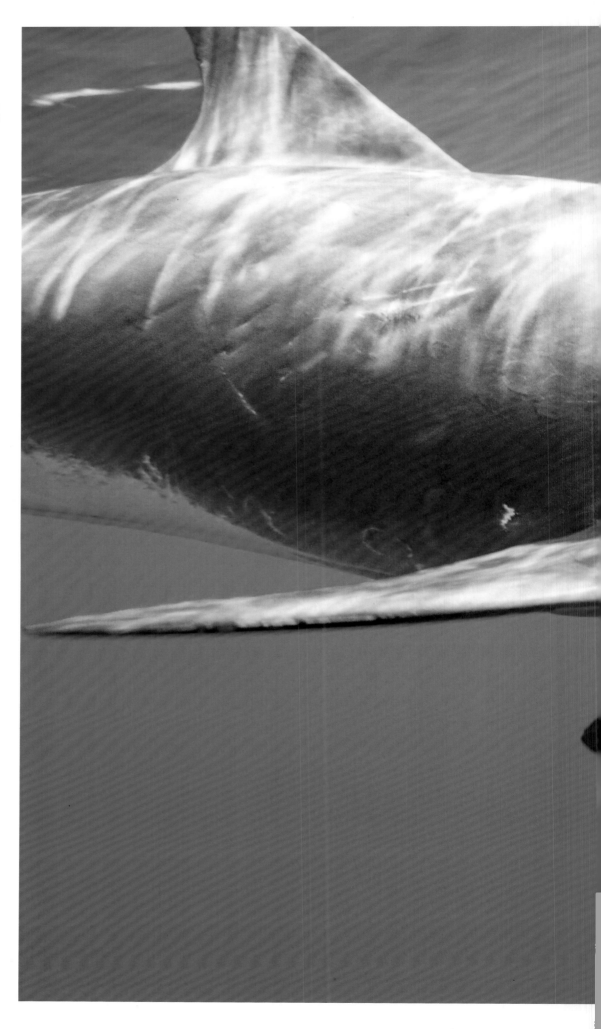

ALL PHOTOGRAPHS:
In hot water
The pygmy killer whale lives in tropical and subtropical waters, and it is a common sight off Pacific islands like Hawaii. The species is gregarious and lives in pods of up to 30 individuals. It is a slow swimmer and seems to prefer to hunt in deeper waters.

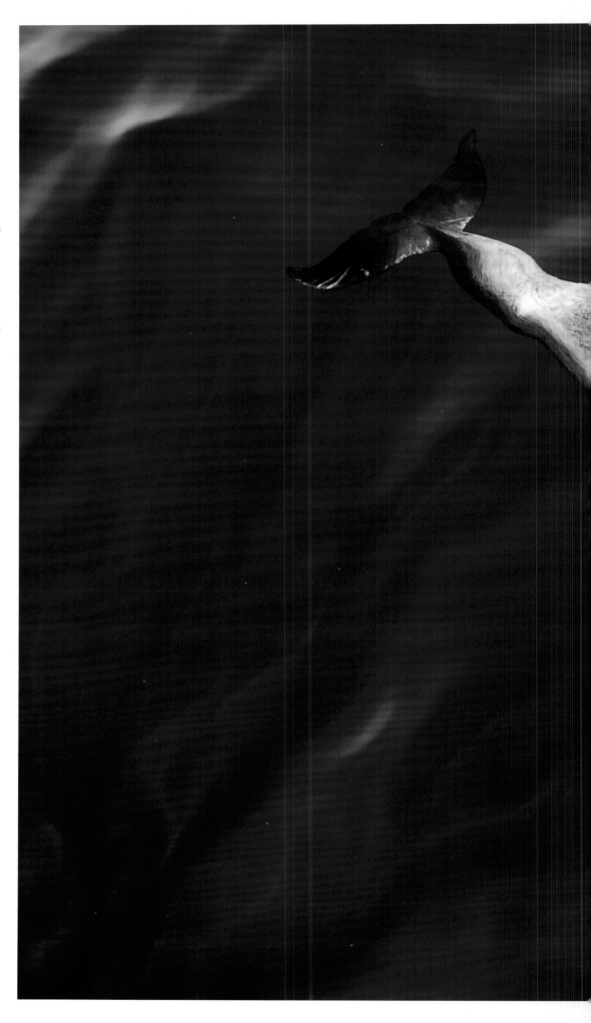

RIGHT:
Risso's dolphin
This unusual dolphin seems to be related to the pilot whales. It lives in many parts of the ocean, mostly in coastal water or above the continental slopes, where the shallow seabed plunges down to the abyss of the open ocean. It is least commonly found in the Atlantic Ocean.

OVERLEAF ALL PHOTOGRAPHS:
Scar face
The feature that marks out Risso's dolphin against the rest is the big rounded head covered in pale scars. These scars run along the back and sides of the body as well and are the result of social interactions – mostly male-on-male conflicts. The dolphin's skins does not recolour these wounds, and this may be an evolved trait where a body covered in obvious scars is a signal of dominance.

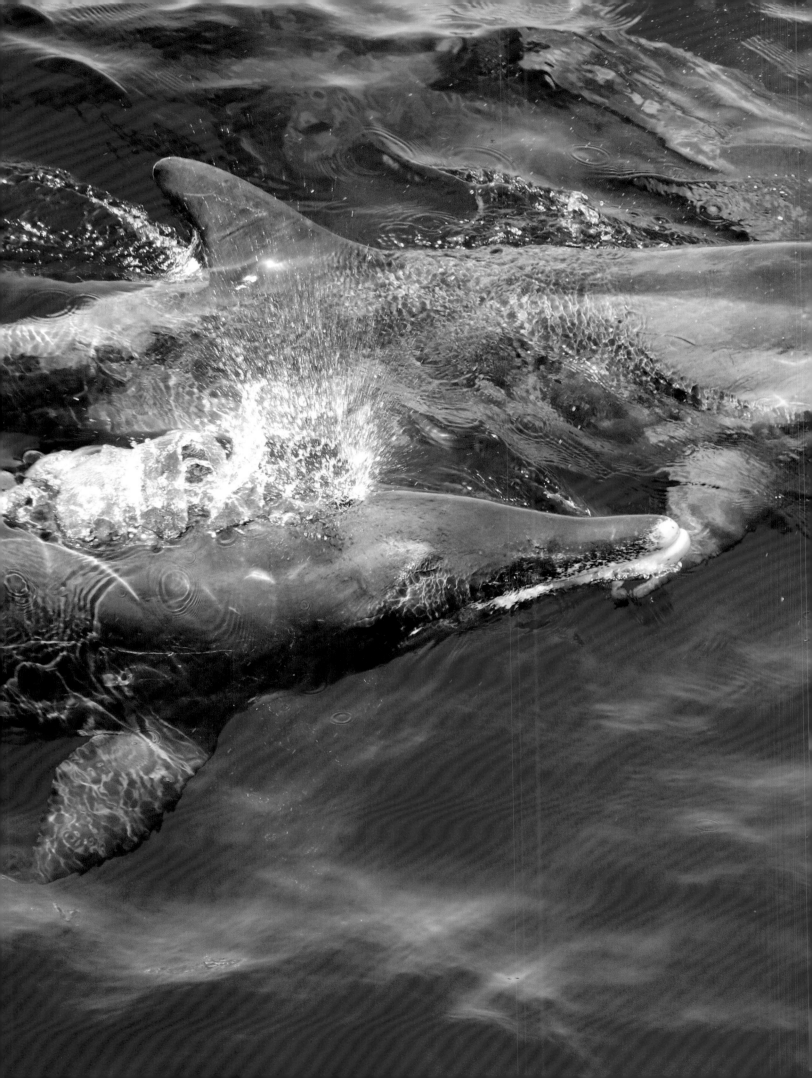

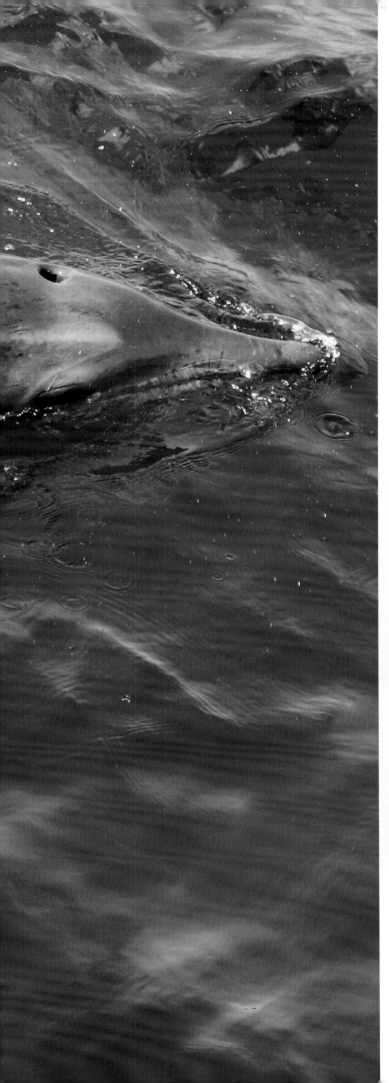

ALL PHOTOGRAPHS:

Rough-toothed dolphin

This large dolphin lives in warm waters worldwide. It has a distinctive narrow beak and sleek head without the pronounced bulging melon seen in many other dolphins. As the name suggests, the teeth are more jagged than the usual peg-like dolphin teeth. This helps with holding small fish prey.

ALL PHOTOGRAPHS:
Short-finned pilot whale
A close relative of the cold-water long-finned pilot whale, this dolphin species lives in the world's temperate and tropical waters. They are highly social dolphins, living in a tight-knit pod where the young are closely protected.

White-beaked dolphin
A specialist feeder on white fish, such as cod and haddock, this species lives in the North Atlantic and Arctic Oceans. They often join the hunts of killer whales picking up the strays or flow humpbacks to snatch up the fish that escape the bubble nets.

ABOVE TOP:
White-beaked dolphin
This is a big species, with some males growing to more than 3m (9.8ft) long. The reason for the common name is plain to see.

ABOVE BOTTOM:
Southern right whale dolphin
This predominantly Antarctic species has much more white on its belly than its northern relation. It makes quite the sight when hundreds of these dolphins congregate.

RIGHT:
Spinner dolphin
This is a small and widespread off-shore species that lives in warmer parts of the oceans. Its name refers to its habit of rolling longitudinally – or spinning – in midair during leaps and breaches.

Striped dolphin

Although it does not like to frequent inshore waters and so is not a common sight, this medium-sized species is one of the most widespread dolphins. Even so, it is absent from the eastern Pacific, where it has been hunted and persecuted by fishermen in the past.

Tucuxi

This endangered species is a
member of the oceanic dolphin
family, but it spends much of its
time deep in the freshwater river
systems of South America. As well
as the huge Amazon basin, the
tucuxi is also seen occasionally in
the Orinoco. The species is under
threat in part because it is hunted
by local people who believe its skin
has medicinal qualities.

Other Toothed Whales

There is a lot more to cetaceans than whales and dolphins. The dolphins belong to a wider group called the toothed whales, or the Odontoceti. This group contains the porpoises, more on which soon, but there is also a mixed bag of other species. Chief among them is the sperm whale, so named for the especially valuable oil this species offered whalers of old. They had to work for it; the sperm whale is the world's largest predator and was known to destroy the puny vessels of its tormentors from time to time. Moby Dick, the famed fictional leviathan, was a sperm whale, and its story was inspired in part by true events.

Also included as toothed whales are the beaked whales (and bottlenosed whales), which are 24 species in the family Ziphiidae. Here, the toothed whale gambit begins to wobble, because although the beaked whales have long snouts, not too dissimilar to a dolphin's, they are largely toothless and rely on sucking up their foods rather than biting hold of them. Beaked whales are bigger than dolphins and seldom seen because they are busy in deep water far out of sight.

Finally, the toothed whales include the Monodontidae. Latin scholars will spot this reads like a family of one-toothed creatures. In fact, one member is the narwhal, whose lone spiralled tusk is the closest natural object to a supernatural unicorn's horn – and the animals were indeed hunted for this reason. The other member of this family is the beluga. While tuskless, this whistling white whale is nevertheless well known, as it is one of the few whale species able to be kept in captivity.

OPPOSITE:
Big sucker
The beluga's small teeth, which are easily worn and lost entirely, are of little use in feeding. The whale sucks in its fishy prey instead.

ABOVE:

White whale

Adult belugas have bright white skin, while the younger whales are a darker grey-blue. The name "beluga" means "white" in Russian.

RIGHT:

No fin

Being white helps the whale blend in among growlers (small icebergs) along the edges of the white sea ice. The dorsal fin is reduced to a ridge to make it easier for the whale to slide along under the ice.

Melon

The beluga has an especially bulbous head. This is in part a flexible oily mass called the melon, which is used to focus the whale's echolocation calls into tight beams suitable for scanning the immediate surroundings. The echoes bouncing back give the whale a picture of what is out there. The beluga often feeds on fast-moving prey in dark waters, so relies a lot on this sense.

Fish food
Belugas hunt near the seabed and prey on large fish, tackling targets one at a time. They have a more flexible neck than any other cetacean, so they can swivel the head and mouth to grab prey. Fish are sucked into the mouth and crushed by the peg-like teeth.

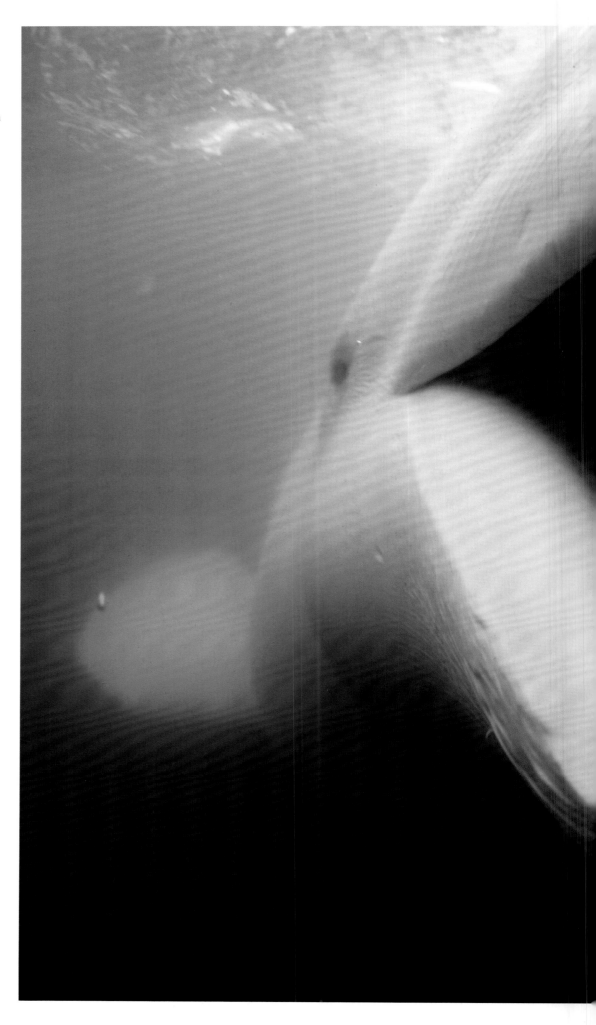

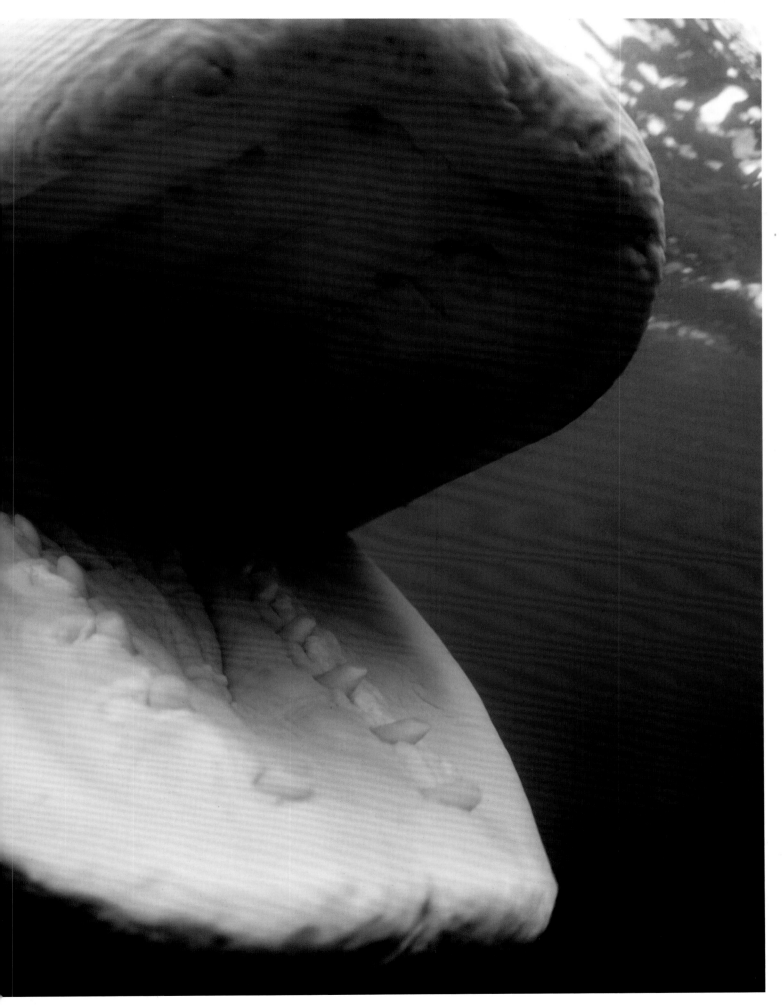

Mass gathering
Belugas follow the edge of the ice as it recedes and grows each year. In the depths of summer, when ice has largely gone, they may head into shallow coastal waters. While they are normally found in small groups, occasionally vast superpods of hundreds of whales form at meeting points along the migration routes.

Winter coat
During the coldest time of winter, the whale's skin thickens and becomes more yellow. This thermal layer becomes irritating in spring, and the whale moves to shallow waters with gravel seabeds, where it writhes on the bottom to rub off the yellow coating.

ABOVE:
Whistlers
The beluga is the most vocal of the whales – at least within the range of human hearing. They produce clear lilting whistle tones that earn them the nickname of "sea canary".

OVERLEAF:
Underwater birth
A beluga calf's tail is emerging from its mother's birth canal. Soon, the newborn whale will be out in the water, and its mother will swiftly steer the calf to the surface for its first breath.

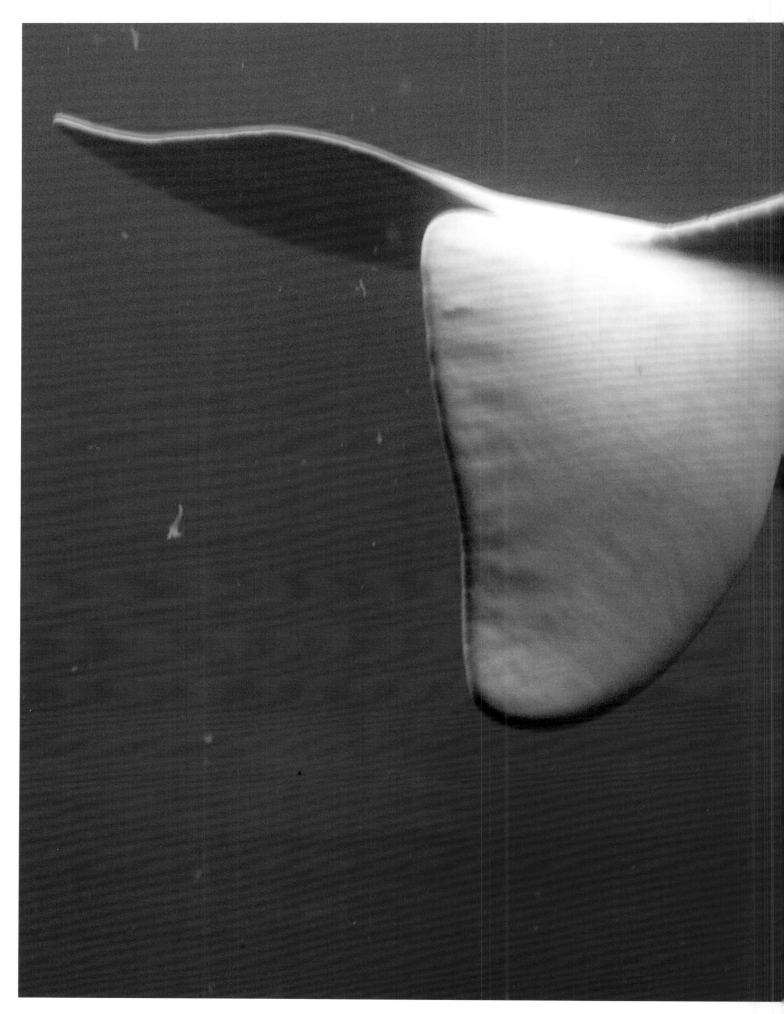

Mother and child
At birth beluga calves are generally
dark gray to bluish or brownish
gray, becoming darker at about
one month. Like other whales,
beluga calves swim at birth. Young
belugas learn survival behaviors by
observing and mimicking adults
in their pod.

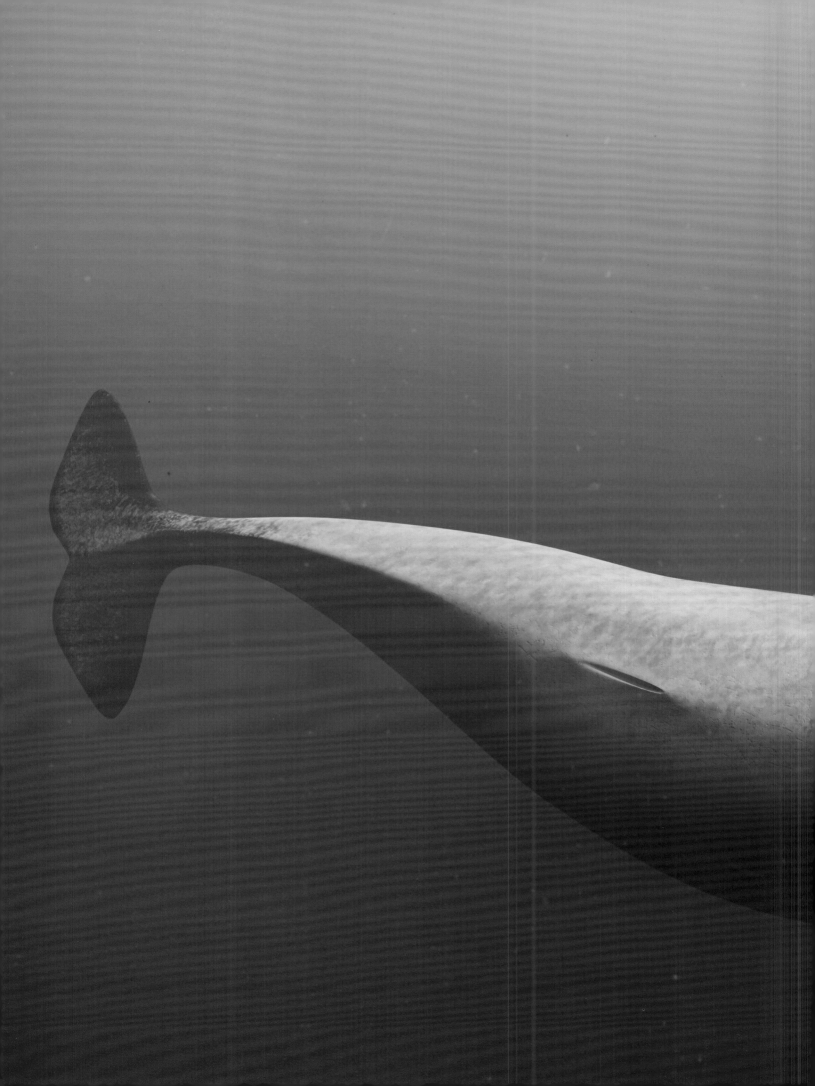

Big tusker
The narwhal is a close cousin of the beluga, matching it in size. However, there is another obvious difference. Males (and a few females) have an enormous spiralled front tooth growing from the top lip into a 2m (6.6ft) tusk. Once assumed to be a weapon, the tooth is not that tough and is now thought more likely to signal good health and be a super-sensitive organ, perhaps detecting chemicals and water currents.

In deep water

The narwhal spends most of its time further out to sea than the white whale, targeting shoaling fish like halibut and cod. It slurps up prey with a sucking action that it has in common with the beaked whales. In summer, the narwhals swim closer to land as coastal ice recedes and may gather in large groups of several dozen.

Following leads
Narwhals spend winter under the thick ice, popping up to breathe in natural gaps and cracks known as leads. It has been postulated that when males meet, they rub tusks to exchange chemical cues that provide information on what waters each animal has swum through recently.

Deep dive
In the summer, the narwhals spend more time in shallow water but follow their food to deeper waters come the winter. During the winter, these animals will be making some of the deepest dives of any mammal, plunging down to 1500m (4921ft) below the surface and staying down for half an hour. They make this journey 15 times a day!

LEFT:
Northern bottlenose whale
This squid-eating beaked whale spends long periods hunting in deep water far out to sea, so it is seldom seen and little understood. While rivalling minke whales in length, the beaked whales are hefty relatives of the dolphins, as their distinctive snouts will attest.

ABOVE TOP:
Sowerby's beaked whale
This 5m (16.4ft) North Atlantic species will pop up to watch passing boats but seldom strays close to the shore. It has also been found in the Mediterranean Sea.

ABOVE BOTTOM:
Arnoux's beaked whale
A resident of the Southern Ocean, this beaked whale ventures north to the waters around New Zealand and south of Australia and comes up the coast of South America beyond the River Plate.

LEFT:

Baird's beaked whale

At around 12m (39.4ft) in length, this is one of the largest beaked whales. It lives in the northern Pacific. The beak is largely toothless. Deep-sea squid are sucked into the mouth, not snapped up. However, the whale has a few teeth remaining for use in fights over mates.

ABOVE TOP AND BOTTOM:

Gervais's beaked whale

Beaked whales appear especially prone to problems caused by human activities. This North Atlantic species is often found with plastic bags in its stomach, which it mistakes for food. Additionally, sonar and engine noises interfere with the echolocation these deep-sea hunters rely on to hunt in dark depths. This disruption may be linked to beaching, where whales becomes trapped in shallow waters and die of exhaustion.

ALL PHOTOGRAPHS:

Blainville's beaked whale

One of the most widespread of the beaked whales, this species prefers temperate and tropical waters. At less than 5m (16.4ft) long, it is smaller than its cold-water cousins but is still adapted to the same deep-sea foraging. When it comes across fish or squid, it springs open the mouth and expands the throat, thus creating an inward rush of water that pulls the food in with it.

Cuvier's beaked whale
Also called the goose-beaked whale, this medium-sized species is the most cosmopolitan of the beaked whales, found in all seas bar the coldest polar waters. This one appears to have had a recent injury, perhaps inflicted by a large squid or a collision with a boat.

ALL PHOTOGRAPHS:
Sperm whale
Large cetaceans such as sperm whales play their part in fertilising the surface of the ocean. They feed in the deep sea and then return to the surface to defecate – transporting the nutrients to contribute to ocean poductivity and the drawdown of atmospheric carbon.

Sperm whale

A diver swims between a female sperm whale and her cub in the waters off the Caribbean island of Dominica. The whales gather here to calve and mate. The mother is eyeing the camera. The fist-sized eye is the largest of any toothed whale and is used to seek squid in the deep.

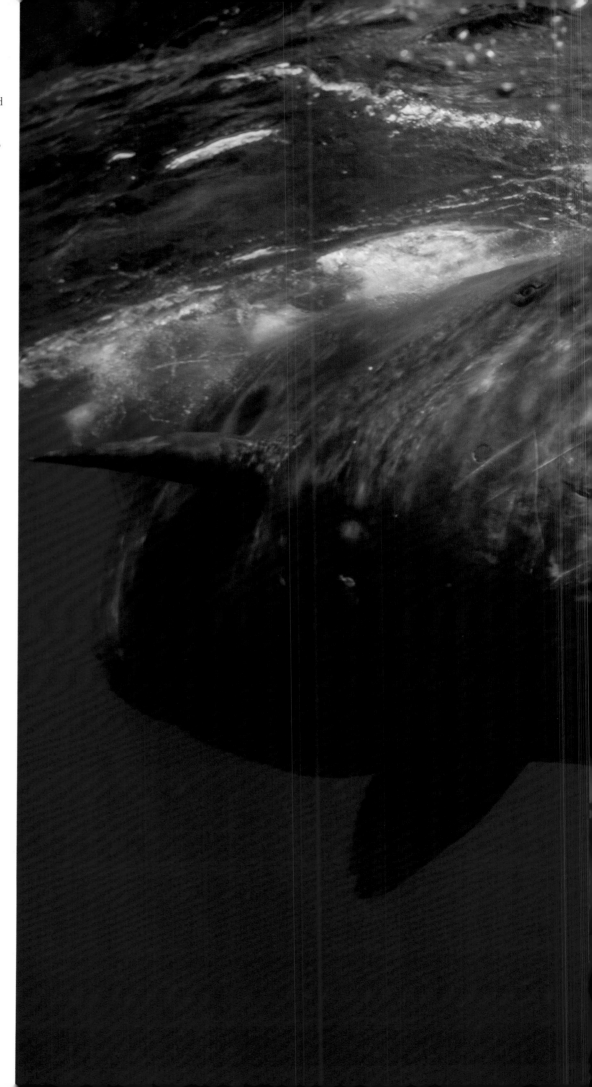

Block head

The sperm whale has a very distinctive look. At 12m (39.4ft) long, it is easily the largest toothed whale, and coupled with the almost cuboid head, which takes up a third of the body, it is hard to mistake this monster for anything else. The narrow jaw, lined with 20-odd 1kg (2.2lb) cone-shaped teeth, is there for snatching giant squid. This prey lives in the midnight zone, down so deep it is dark 24 hours a day. The sperm whale uses its immense squared-up melon to echolocate its preferred food on long dives that take it more than 2km (1.2 miles) underwater for two hours at a time.

OPPOSITE:
Feeding time
A sperm whale can live for 70 years and starts breeding around the age of 10. A calf is produced every five years or so until the females go through a menopause in their forties. Older whales are crucial for successful breeding in that they protect the mother and calf from attack during the early weeks after birth.

LEFT:
Shallow sleep
Sperm whales sleep vertically in the water with the head just below the surface. They sleep for about four hours at a time, mostly in the late evening.

Global travellers
Sperm whales live in all oceans in the parts that are more than 1000m (3281ft) deep and ice-free at the surface. The population was reduced by two-thirds by whaling ships, which saw more than a million of these creatures killed for their oil before whaling was banned in the 1980s. There are now thought to be 300,000 spread across the oceans today.

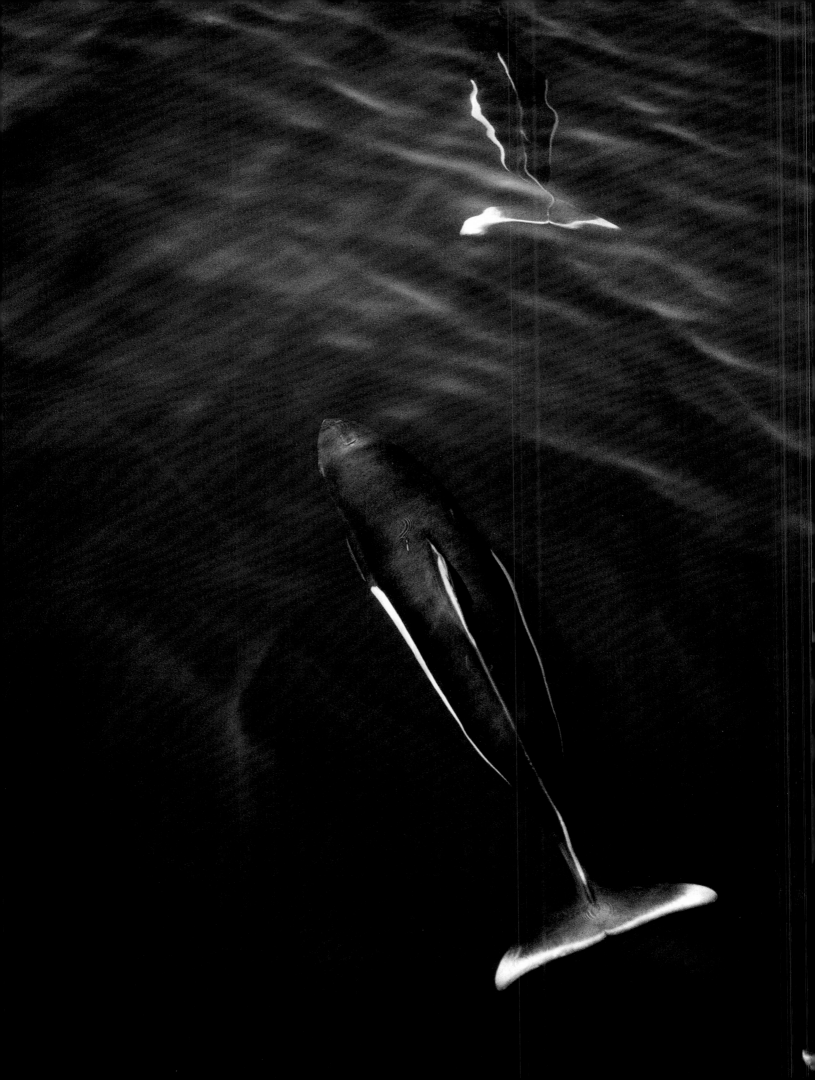

Porpoises

Pity the porpoises. These most diminutive of the cetaceans are so often overlooked. They are mostly lumped in with the dolphins, despite being a closer relation to the narwhal and beluga. The dolphins have even grabbed attention for the one thing that porpoises stand out for: porpoising. This is the swimming technique where the animal makes rhythmic leaps into the air. This allows the animal to breathe steadily while maintaining a high speed through the water.

Seen from afar, a porpoising porpoise could be mistaken for a dolphin by the uninitiated. However, these eight species, all contained within the family Phocoenidae, have distinctive rounded faces. There is no beak or nose-like snout. This is not definitive because there are some similarly snub-nosed dolphins too. Another clue is that porpoises have flatter, spade-shaped teeth, contrasting with the pointed cones of dolphin teeth. Invariably, a porpoise will be the smaller animal in a matchup with other cetaceans. The largest, Dall's porpoise, is barely more than 2m (6.6ft) long, while the tiny vaquita – almost certain to be extinct soon, with only 10 left in the wild – is only 140cm (55.1in) long.

The Phocoenidae has three tribes. One is occupied by Dall's porpoise, another by the true porpoises (like the vaquita) and the third by the finless porpoises. These coastal species from South and East Asia lack a dorsal fin. The porpoises tend to live in shallow coastal seas, and more than half of them are endangered.

Black and white
Dall's porpoise can have an all-white or all-black body but most show both colours. The most common pattern is a black back with white stripes on the side and belly, as seen here.

Dall's porpoise hunts mostly at night. This is when predatory fish, squid and crustaceans are migrating upwards from deep dark waters to feast on the plankton near the surface. The porpoise targets these nighttime raiders.

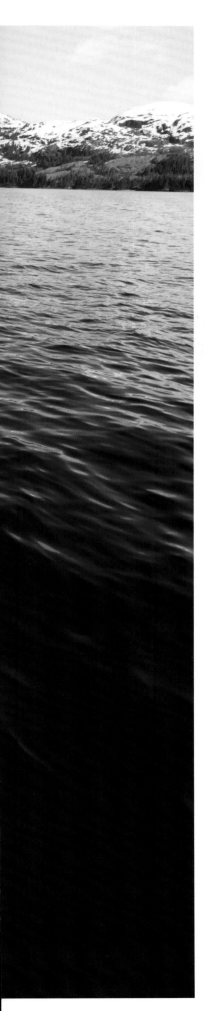

LEFT:
Waver running
Dall's porpoise seems very friendly to, or at least curious about, humans in the water. It often comes along for the ride, surfing the bow waves of fast boats. It is the fastest porpoise, capable of speeds of 55km/h (34.2mph).

ABOVE TOP:
Indo-Pacific finless porpoise
Named for its lack of dorsal fin, this species hugs the coasts from the Persian Gulf to the islands of Indonesia. It eats a wide range of fish and shellfish and even munches on plants when straying into river mouths.

ABOVE BOTTOM:
Yangtze finless porpoise
This is the only freshwater species of porpoise, and after the reported extinction of the baiji, or Yangtze river dolphin, it is China's only freshwater cetacean left.

ALL PHOTOGRAPHS:

Harbour porpoise
This is the most widespread porpoise species. It swims in the coastal waters of the North Pacific from the Sea of Japan to the Beaufort Sea and Northern California. In the North Atlantic, it is seen from along the Eastern Seaboard of North America to Iceland, in the Laptev Sea and down the coast of West Africa. There is even a relict population living in the Black Sea.

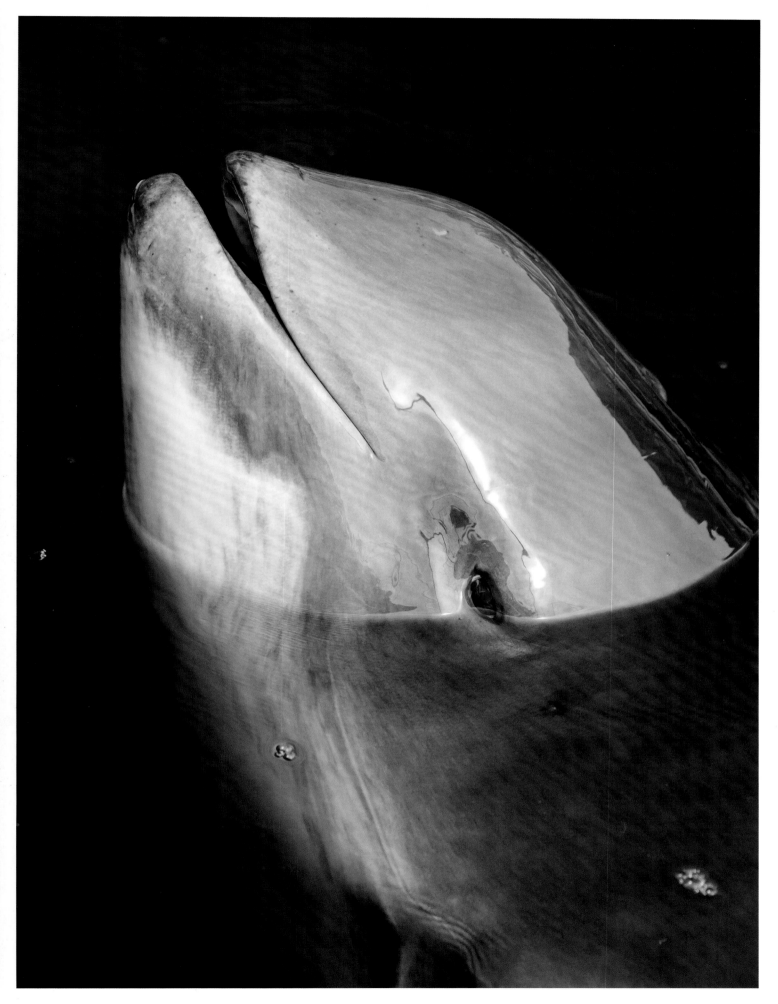

Stay shallow
The harbour porpoise seldom strays into water deeper than around 200m (656ft). It feeds near the bottom and targets fish, such as herrings and sprats.

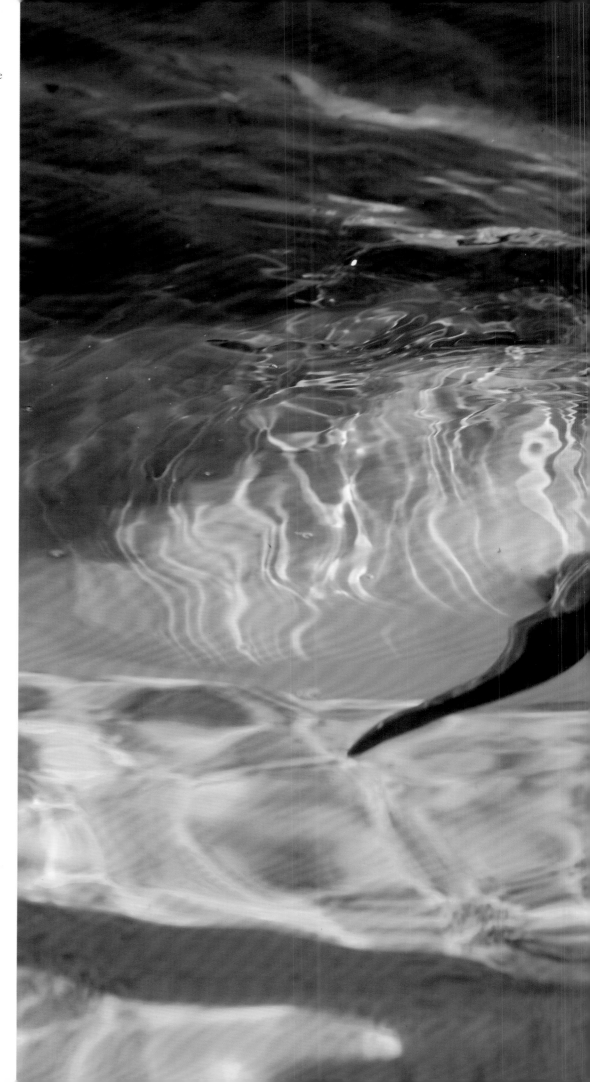

Simple life
The harbour porpoise tends to live a solitary existence and appears not to be nomadic. Instead, each individual will spend its whole life – perhaps 15 years – in a home territory.

In danger
The harbour porpoise is an endangered species. Its main threat is from fishing nets because it frequents some of the world's most intensive fisheries. Once tangled in a net, the porpoise is unable to surface to breathe and will drown within minutes. Some nets are fitted with pingers that scare the animals away, but these are proving less effective as the porpoises become used to them.

Picture Credits